FunTime® Piano

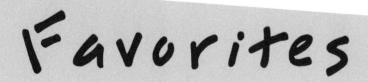

Favorites

Level 3A-3B

Easy Piano

This book belongs to: _____

T0057121

Arranged by

Nancy and Randall Faber

Production: Frank and Gail Hackinson
Production Coordinator: Marilyn Cole
Cover: Terpstra Design, San Francisco
Engraving: Tempo Music Press, Inc.

FABER
PIANO ADVENTURES®
3042 Creek Drive
Ann Arbor, Michigan 48108

A NOTE TO TEACHERS

FunTime® Piano Favorites presents traditional, ever-popular melodies in pianistic arrangements for the early intermediate piano student. Selections include the melodic *Skaters' Waltz* and *Scarborough Fair*, as well as timeless favorites such as *I've Been Working on the Railroad* and *Song of the Volga Boatmen*.

Pieces are in the keys of C, G, F, A minor and D minor, and feature a variety of sounds. The pieces may be assigned in any order according to the student interest.

FunTime® Piano Favorites designates Level 3A–3B of the *PreTime®* to *BigTime®* *Piano Supplementary Library* arranged by Faber and Faber.

Following are the levels of the supplementary library, which lead from *PreTime®* to *BigTime®.*

PreTime® Piano	(Primer Level)
PlayTime® Piano	(Level 1)
ShowTime® Piano	(Level 2A)
ChordTime® Piano	(Level 2B)
FunTime® Piano	(Level 3A – 3B)
BigTime® Piano	(Level 4)

Each level offers books in a variety of styles, making it possible for the teacher to offer stimulating material for every student. For a complimentary detailed listing, e-mail faber@pianoadventures.com or write us at the mailing address listed below.

Visit **www.PianoAdventures.com**.

Helpful Hints:

1. Hands-alone practice is very helpful.

2. The melodic nature of the selections offers opportunity for the teacher to stress balance between the hands.

3. Students who wish to sing should be encouraged to do so. Others may wish to accompany a friend or family member who sings.

4. For a rewarding ensemble experience, the melodies can be played by an instrumentalists while the student plays along.

ISBN 978-1-61677-054-9

Copyright © 1997 by Dovetree Productions, Inc.
c/o FABER PIANO ADVENTURES, 3042 Creek Dr., Ann Arbor, MI 48108
International Copyright Secured.   All Rights Reserved.   Printed in U.S.A.
WARNING: The music, text, design, and graphics in this publication are protected by copyright law.
Any duplication is an infringement of U.S. copyright law.

TABLE OF CONTENTS

Greensleeves

Traditional English

This arrangement © 1996 by Dovetree Productions, Inc., c/o FABER PIANO ADVENTURES.
International Copyright Secured.   All Rights Reserved.

Give My Regards to Broadway

Words and Music by
George M. Cohan

This arrangement © 1996 by Dovetree Productions, Inc., c/o FABER PIANO ADVENTURES.
International Copyright Secured.   All Rights Reserved.

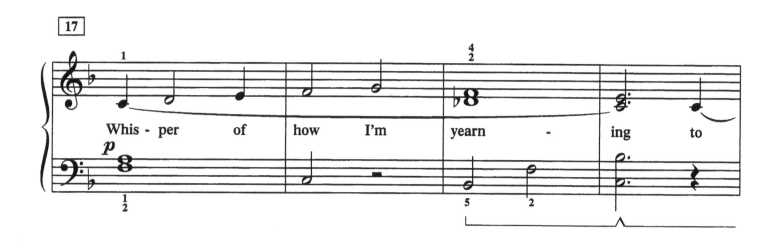

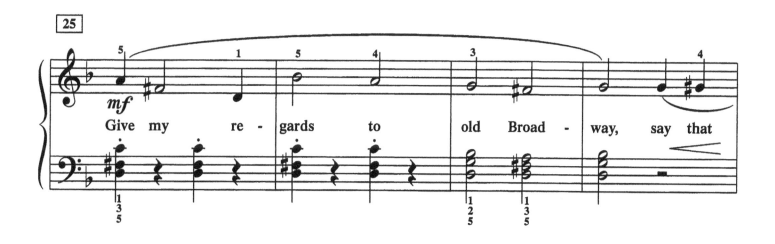

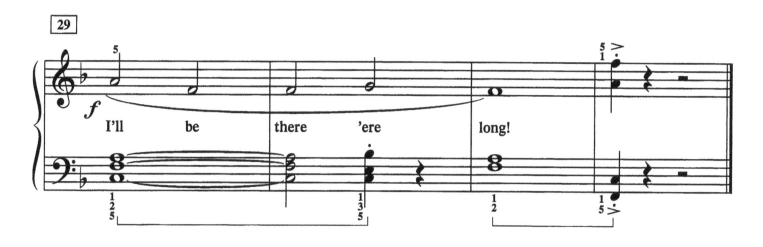

Song of the Volga Boatmen

Traditional Russian

This arrangement © 1996 by Dovetree Productions, Inc., c/o FABER PIANO ADVENTURES.
International Copyright Secured.   All Rights Reserved.

Hello, My Baby

Traditional ragtime

This arrangement © 1996 by Dovetree Productions, Inc., c/o FABER PIANO ADVENTURES.
International Copyright Secured.   All Rights Reserved.

then you'll be left a - lone. Oh, ba - by, tele - phone and

tell me I'm your own!

Fine

D.C. al Fine

FF1054

Scarborough Fair

Traditional English

This arrangement © 1996 by Dovetree Productions, Inc., c/o FABER PIANO ADVENTURES.
International Copyright Secured.   All Rights Reserved.

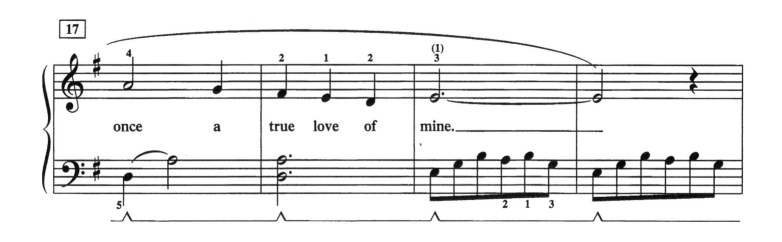

once a true love of mine.

Tell her to make me a cam - bric shirt,

mf

(p)

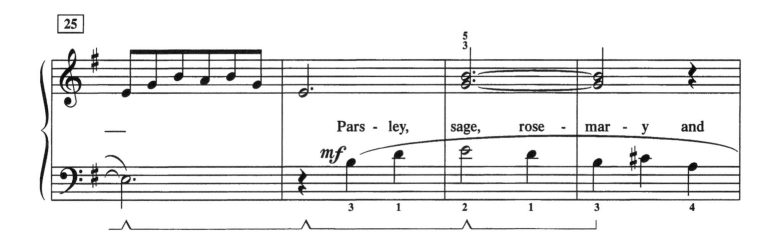

Pars - ley, sage, rose - mar - y and

mf

thyme; with - out seams or

(p) *mf*

14

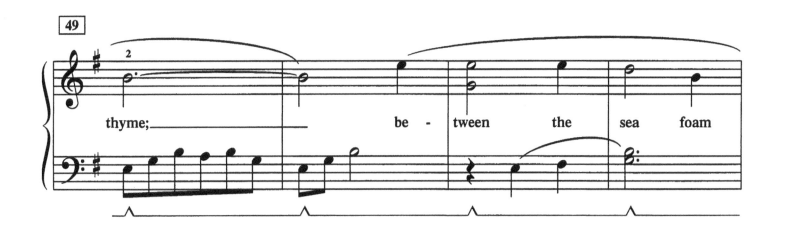

thyme;_____ be - tween the sea foam

and the sea sand,_____ or

he'll not be a true love of mine.

mp *rit.* *a tempo* *p*

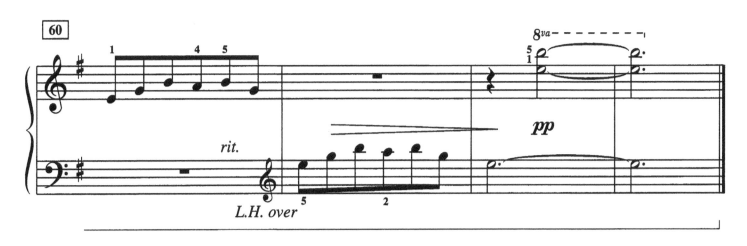

rit. *pp*

L.H. over

The Arkansas Traveler

Traditional U.S.

This arrangement © 1996 by Dovetree Productions, Inc., c/o FABER PIANO ADVENTURES.
International Copyright Secured.   All Rights Reserved.

Glow Worm

Paul Lincke

This arrangement © 1996 by Dovetree Productions, Inc., c/o FABER PIANO ADVENTURES.
International Copyright Secured.   All Rights Reserved.

Two Guitars

Traditional

This arrangement © 1996 by Dovetree Productions, Inc., c/o FABER PIANO ADVENTURES.
International Copyright Secured.   All Rights Reserved.

22

FF1054

I've Been Working on the Railroad

Traditional U.S.

This arrangement © 1996 by Dovetree Productions, Inc., c/o FABER PIANO ADVENTURES.
International Copyright Secured.   All Rights Reserved.

25

The Skaters' Waltz

Emile Charles Waldteufel

Graceful waltz tempo

This arrangement © 1996 by Dovetree Productions, Inc., c/o FABER PIANO ADVENTURES.
International Copyright Secured.   All Rights Reserved.

Chopsticks

Traditional

This arrangement © 1996 by Dovetree Productions, Inc., c/o FABER PIANO ADVENTURES.
International Copyright Secured.   All Rights Reserved.

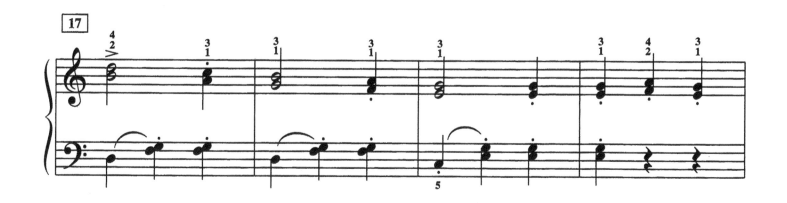

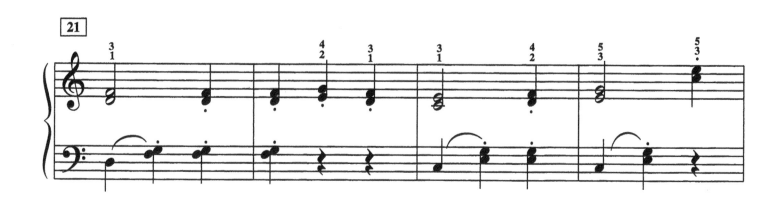

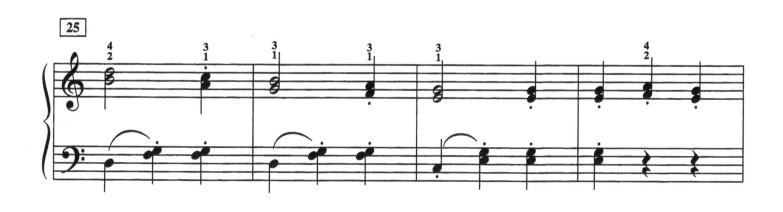

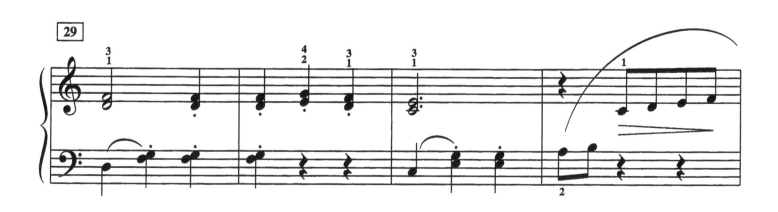

32

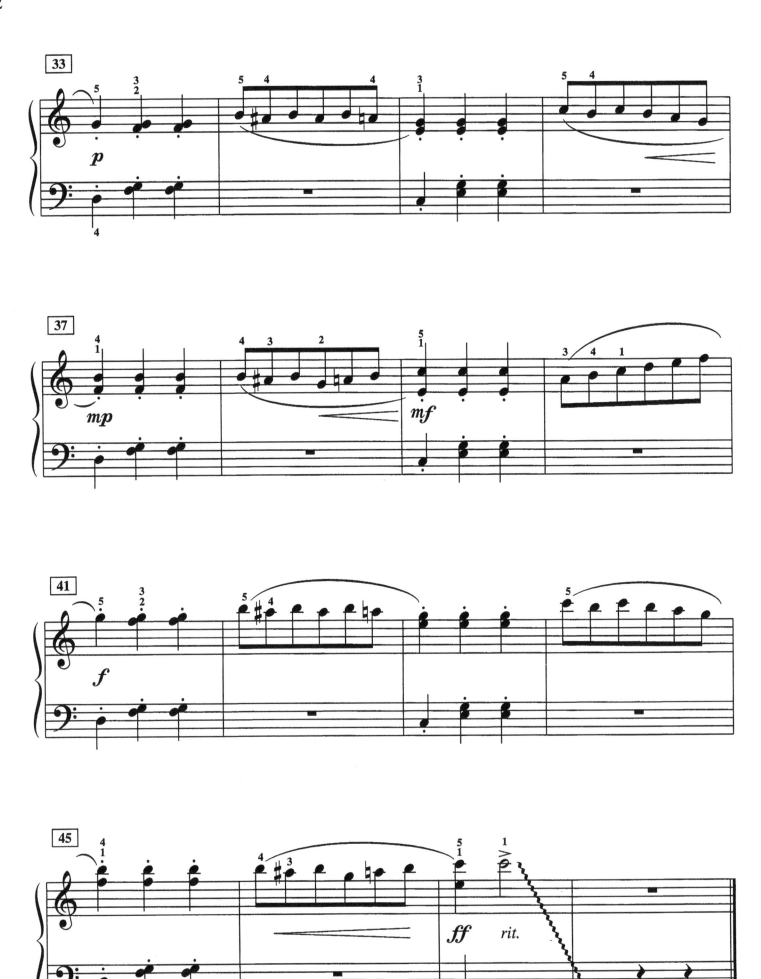